T0147567

IN THE NAME OF
JESUS
I PRAY

Donovan O. Brown

iUniverse, Inc.
New York   Bloomington

In the Name of Jesus I Pray

iUniverse books may be ordered through booksellers or by contacting:

iUniverse
1663 Liberty Drive
Bloomington, IN 47403
www.iuniverse.com
1-800-Authors (1-800-288-4677)

ISBN: 978-1-4401-2110-4 (sc)
ISBN: 978-1-4401-2111-1 (ebk)

Printed in the United States of America

iUniverse rev. date: 02/23/2009

Jesus my Lord and Almighty God

I believe and declare that nothing is impossible

for you to accomplish.

Lord Jesus, I ask you in the name of Jesus to invade the

kingdom of darkness and evil and invade the lives of

your people who are lost in that kingdom and speak to

them. Give them revelation about you and what you

have done for us all. Lord change their lives by

renewing their minds and bring them in your kingdom.

Rescue them my Lord from the clutches of evil, death

and hell.

Do this now my God in the name of Jesus I ask and pray.

Amen

Jesus my Lord and friend, my life is in turmoil as I speak. My heart is filled with fear and my mind confused with worry.

Lord I turn to you and no one else for help. For you have the power to help, to save and to deliver me. You Lord are my help and strength and my hope in you will not be disappointed.

Lord you never promised a life on earth without pain or hardship but you have promised to be with me even in the darkest of times. Lord this is a dark chapter in my life and all my cares I rest on you. I know you are with me and even though I do not see you, I know you are working on my behalf to resolve all my troubles.

Thank you Lord Jesus for my victory over these present troubles.

In the name of Jesus I pray and thank you.

Amen

Lord Jesus thank you for ordering my steps out of and
away from danger and for leading me into abundant
blessings.

Lord you are the source of my hope, the source of my
help, the source of my peace, the source of my joy and
the source of every wonderful thing in my life.

Thank you Lord for my family, my job, my home, my car,
my friends and for this and everyday which you give to
me.

In the name of Jesus I pray.

Amen

Lord Jesus thank you for healing my mind and body. Thank you for the grace, peace and mercy which you, Lord, have given to me. You have given me many victories, great opportunities, abundant resources and I have your favour.

Lord Jesus thank you for freeing me from poverty and debt. I know that any weapon or plan that is forged to harm me will never accomplish its purpose, for I have your favour and protection.

All the stumbling blocks which the enemy have brought into my life to stop me from progressing, you Lord Jesus have turned them into stepping stones which will lead me to levels so high I never knew existed.

Thank you Lord for watching over me every step of the way, for your council, for every blessing and every word of encouragement and for being a true friend.

In the name of Jesus I pray.

Amen

Lord Jesus I declare there is nothing impossible for you to accomplish, so Lord I come to you who can do the impossible and appeal to you to let your Holy Spirit descend upon not only this government but every government throughout the world and let your will be done through every one of them.

Let your Holy Spirit invade police forces, schools, local governments and armies throughout this nation and nations throughout the world and let your will be done through them all.

Lord send your Holy Spirit to invade cities, villages, homes and lives all over this world and renew the minds of all who will listen to your instructions and bring all into your kingdom.

In the name of Jesus I ask and pray.

Amen

Jehovah, our heavenly father, please listen to the

prayers and pleas of your people and act now.

Father, you said anyone who calls upon you,

you Lord will answer, help, heal, save, deliver and bless.

Lord let every weapon constructed to harm your people

whether it is to kill, stop or hinder, let them fail.

Condemn every mouth which speaks against your

chosen. Perform miracles and wonders in and through

the lives of your people who have open the door of

their minds and lives to you.

In the name of Jesus I pray.

Amen

Jesus you are Lord over everything in the heavens and you are Lord over everything on earth. You rule everything, from the waves to the depths of the ocean. Everything, even demons in the depths of hell bow to your authority, you are truly Lord over all.

Lord your love for me is so great that you rose from your thrown and left the glory and splendours of heaven to live as a mortal man and suffered and died for me; paying the price of sins I have committed, breaching the gap which separated me from my Father in heaven and seating me in glory with you.

Here I am Lord, the one whom you have saved, the one whom you have purchased with your life and blood. Reveal yourself to me Lord, come in and share my life. In the name of Jesus I pray.

Amen

Jehovah, our heavenly father the whole world is experiencing an economic crisis. Many people are in despair, fear has gripped their hearts.

Thank you for setting my mind at ease; joy fills my heart even now, for it is on you all my cares, my needs and wants I rest. I am your child and you have promised to take care of me and you have cause me to live in abundance of good things even in these darkest days. My obedience to your word Lord, gives you permission to work in my life and do the impossible. In your word there is abundance of life. Thank you Father for being faithful to your word and to me.

It is in the name of Jesus I pray.

Amen.

Jehovah, Almighty God and Father I come to you in the name of Jesus, to thank you for keeping me safe and my mind at peace in this chaotic time. Thank you Lord that I can bring all my concerns and worries to you in prayer. You who have the power and authority to put all things right. Father thank you for holding my marriage and my family together.

Father you are my refuge in times of danger, my provider in my times of need and my councillor in times of uncertainty and confusion. Thank you Father for everything, it is in Jesus name I pray.

Amen

Holy Spirit move upon the people of the true and living

God; as you had done on the day of Pentecost.

Move upon us now in your power and authority,

and through us do the impossible.

Holy Spirit bring us un-natural success and amaze the

world. Speak to our hearts and change our lives and

manifest yourself in us.

In the name of Jesus I ask and pray.

Amen

Lord Jesus, bring peace where there is turmoil, healing where there is injury or pain. Bring joy where there is sorrow, hope where there is despair, wealth where there is poverty.

Lord we need you always, never leave us or forsake us, forgive and remove our sins far from us. Help us to walk in your will and your word, be patient with us Lord. We love you always and look to you for help. Thank you for bringing peace, joy, victory and your blessings to our lives. In the name of Jesus I pray and thank you Lord.

Amen

Lord Jesus, you have promised to bless all which I do.

So Lord, please crown my works with success as

you have promised. As I have been faithful to your

word Lord, please open the windows of heaven and

pour out through them in my life blessings so great I

will not have room enough in my life to contain them

all.

Remember your promises and bless me now, Lord.

I need the blessing which you have promised.

In the name of Jesus I ask and pray.

Amen

Lord Jesus, I am financially prosperous, I have a
wonderful and healthy family, a fabulous business / job,
My life is overflowing with good things, everything is
going well, but Lord I feel far from you.
As you have said, "what does it profit a man to gain the
whole world but at the same time lose his soul."
Lord invade my life and fill this emptiness, bridge the
distance between us.
Lord you said, "Behold, I stand at the door, and knock:
if any man hears my voice, and opens the door, I will
come in to him, and will eat with him, and he with me."
Lord you are knocking at the door of my heart; enter
Lord.
Lord Jesus, my life, my hope, my future and my desires,
I place all in your hands, in your power, in your
authority.
In the name of Jesus I pray.
Amen

Father you are literally the source of my life and
strength. Thank you for always being a my defence and
for always fighting my battles which always result in
victory even when I do not get my desired result, for I
know there can be victory in defeat.
Thank you for your unrestrained love which you have
lavished upon me even before my birth into your
kingdom.
You have promised that nothing in heaven on earth or
under the earth, not even past or future sins can
separate me from your love which you have freely
given.
Father thank you for the grace, peace, mercy, joy and
hope which comes from your love to my life.
In the name of Jesus I pray.
Amen

Abba Father, thank you for your protection,

grace, mercy, favour and love. Without you Father I

would be lost in the world of darkness fill with hatred

and fear.

Thank you Father for rescuing me from that world

and its ways of thinking. I need your presence always

and the encouragement of your Holy Spirit.

In the name of Jesus your son I pray.

Amen

Lord Jesus I am a very blessed man, my life overflows

with the blessings which continuously pouring

in and I thank you Lord for blessing me so greatly.

Now Lord I need your help to overcome these present

hurdles which I now face, these present problems

which have ambushed my life.

Keep me safe Lord, hide me, help me, direct me and

give me your good council. I know you have already

answered my prayers; for you Lord have told me that

you have answered my prayers even before the words

have left my mouth, and I take confidence in your word

and promises.

I will get through these present troubles victoriously,

you have already made a way of escape for me.

It is in your name Lord, in the name of Jesus, I declare

victory over these situations I face.

In the name of Jesus I pray and declare.

Amen

Jehovah, Eternal God and everlasting Father, you have
told me to bring all my concerns to you, so here I lay
them at your feet.

Father I need your divine intervention at my place of
work, for many enemies have arisen against me,
enemies both in the natural and supernatural.

Lord I am fearful, please get involved and deal with
those who are in the spiritual as well as
those in the physical realm.

I leave them as well as myself in your power and
I thank you, right now in advance for the victory
over those who have risen against me.

In the name of Jesus I pray and thank you Lord.

Amen

Lord Jesus, I need your help and direction, I am

frustrated and do not know where to go or what to do.

Lord what should I do with my life?

What path should I take?

Help me Lord, I do not want to waste my life, help me to

exploit all the talents which you have deposited within

me.

Give me ideas and direction, create opportunities so

that I can improve and advance in life greatly.

Hear my prayer for help and act now Lord Jesus.

In the name of Jesus I pray.

Amen

Lord Jesus what you have done for me proves that you love me. Thank you Lord for where you have brought me from. I was lost in the word of evil and your Holy Spirit invaded my life and spoke to me and helped me to change my way of thinking which changed my life for better and have brought me into your kingdom.

All I have and where I am is because of you Lord. You have manifested yourself in your power within me, Lord Jesus I ask you, to do the same for others as you have done for me out of your compassion and love.

In the name of Jesus I ask and pray.

Amen

Lord Jesus no idle word ever leaves your mouth and whatever you say must come into reality.

Lord you have promised to pour out your Holy Spirit upon all flesh in the last days. Lord Jesus these are the last days, so pour out your Holy Spirit, Lord, on everyone over the world as you have said.

Let your Holy Spirit heal lives, relationships, homes and families. Let your spirit bring peace, victory, hope, joy, love and revelation knowledge about you to all peoples.

Act now my God in the name of Jesus I ask and pray.

Amen

Jesus, Lord God almighty, you said, "Many will say to Me in that day, 'Lord, Lord, have we not prophesied in Your name, cast out demons in Your name, and done many wonders in Your name?'

And then you will say to them, "'Depart from Me, I never knew you...'"

Lord there are many who follow the rituals of religion rather than you. Help me not to fall into that crowd, but rather help me to be someone who is truly connected to you. It is better to be favoured by you rather than man.

Lord Jesus, help me to do the will of the Father in heaven so that you will say to me well done good and faithful servant.

And Lord please do not forget those who truly love you but who have been captured by the deceptions of religion. Lord Jesus descend upon them in your power and open   their spiritual eyes and set them free.

In the name of Jesus I ask and pray.

Amen

Jesus my Lord, you said the life of the flesh is in the
blood. Thank you Lord for your precious blood which
have washed away all my sins.

Lord Jesus, cover me with your blood today. Let your
blood seep deep into my mind and heal me.

Cover my brothers, sisters, my father and my relatives,
family and friends with your precious blood. Let it heal
them and bring them closer to you.

Lord Jesus thank you, for blessing my life with your
presence and the power of your spirit and for
delivering me from the power and plans of my enemies.

Lord Jesus come into my life and take full control and
please forgive me of the sins I have committed.

In the name of Jesus I ask and pray.

Amen

Lord Jesus I have sinned against you, myself and others
and now Lord what I have done has brought trouble in
my life; trouble which I need your help to get out of.
Please forgive me of the sins I have committed Lord
Jesus and help me.

Help me Lord to get out of this mess which my
disobedience and arrogance have landed me into.
Lord heal my marriage, my family and others who
are suffering as a result of my selfish actions.

I come to you Lord because you are my Lord and you
have the power to do the impossible and the ability to
put all things right.

Lord I not only surrender my situation to you but also
myself in your hands.

In the name of Jesus I pray.

Amen

Jehovah my heavenly father,

Hallelujah Almighty God and hallowed be your name.

Father thank you for this day and all its blessings.

You sacrificed your innocent son, Jesus, so that we,

your people would live in peace even in the middle of

the storms which life brings and we would live in

abundance even in times of famine.

Father break down all obstacles be they spiritual,

physical and or mental which hinder your people from

seizing and utilizing the opportunities which you have

provided for us.

You, Father have already forgiven us of the sins we have

committed so Father help us to move forward and to

new heights.

In the name of Jesus I ask and pray.

Amen

Lord Jesus, where are you?

Where are you my God?

You have promised me if I obey your word, you would

deliver me out of my trouble and protect me from all

my and enemies; and you would cause everything I do

to prosper and wherever I would succeed and prosper.

Lord where is the evidence of your promises?

Where is the fulfilment of your promises in my life?

Where are you my Lord Jesus, my God?

Lord, those who reject you and ridicule your word and

your ways are prospering.

Lord Jesus where is the success and prosperity in the

lives of those who love you and seek you?

Where is the prosperity of those who follow and

trust in you even when ridiculed?

Where are you, Lord Jesus? Where are the

manifestations of your promises in the lives of you

people?

Lord Jesus, please honour your word, we your people

need the blessings and mercies, we need your promises

to be manifest in our lives.

It is in the name of Jesus I pray.

Amen

Jehovah, my father and Almighty God,

thank you for forgiving me and setting me free from

the consequences of the sins I have committed.

Father thank you for life and good health which so much

of us take for granted. Thank you for clothing me in a

right state of mind and for my job which occupies my

time and provides me with money so that I can pay my

bills.

Father thank you for my comfortable home and the

good health and wellbeing of my family and friends.

Thank you Father for today and all the abundant

blessings which you have stored in it for me.

It is in the name of Jesus I pray.

Amen

Lord Jesus, come in and change my life Lord.

Stir up the talents which you have deposited in me and cause me to be fruitful. Lord , open doors of great opportunities for me so that I can improve my life and enlarge my territory.

Close doors in my life which needs to be shut and break down barriers which separate me from my blessings and build barriers where they need to be in place.

Lord, help me and direct me; deliver me safely from my enemies who are in the spiritual as well as the natural realms.

In the name of Jesus I pray.

Amen

Lord Jesus thank you for your grace and I ask you for your forgiveness of the sins which I have committed.

Lord thank you for your help and I ask you for your favour.

Lord I thank you for peace even in the middle of a storm and I ask you for your council.

Lord I thank you for your love which you have freely given and I ask you for mercy and protection.

Lord Jesus thank you for being my refuge, my rock, the source my strength and my provider during the difficult times.

Lord thank you for not rejecting me on the account of the many sins I have committed.

You are a faithful God; you are a loving God and I thank you for everything Jesus my Lord.

It is in the name of Jesus that I pray.

Amen

In the name of Jesus I declare victory over all my enemies who have come against me and the problems which I am experiencing.

In the name of Jesus I declare the healing of my body, I declare an abundant increase in my finances, I declare peace, joy, happiness and the abundance of all good things in my life in the name of Jesus.

I declare any weapon constructed to destroy me will not prosper and every tongue that rises against me will fail.

Victory is mine, joy is mine, peace is mine, success is mine in the name of Jesus I declare.

Amen

Jesus, Almighty God and everlasting Father.

There are many people in this world who believe in you

but have distorted views as to who you truly are.

Lord release your Holy Spirit upon everyone of them,

speak to them, give them revelation about who you

truly are.

Let them see that you are not only uncompromising

in righteousness but you are also full of life. Help them

to grow out of their rigid religious and boring mind set

and know you as you truly are.

Teach them so that they can reflect you as you truly are,

a God filled with life, love, joy, mercy and peace.

A God, a Father whom everyone can approach without

fear of condemnation and rejection.

In the name of Jesus I ask and pray.

Amen

Jehovah our Father and God, You told us to think big
and prosperous. You told us to enlarge our thinking, to
think outside our sphere of influence. You told us to
ask you for the radical for nothing is impossible for You
to accomplish and you are able to do exceeding
abundantly above all that we ask or think, according to
your power that works in us and in the world.
You have promised to give us the desires of our heart
and we are to trust in your word, for you are not man
that you should tell a lie.
Father I trust in you and have followed as you
have instructed, I now await the fulfilment of your word
in my life.
Thank you Father, in the name of Jesus I pray.
Amen

Jehovah, my father in heaven, thank you for humbling and making my enemies my footstool as you have promised. Now Father help me to forgive them and not harbour any malice in my heart towards them because of what they have done to me.

Help me Lord to forgive and let go as you have forgiven and have forgotten all the wrongs which I have done, as I myself have hurt others and desired and welcomed your forgiveness.

In Jesus name I pray.

Amen

Lord Jesus there is power and victory in your blood.
I plead the blood of Jesus over my life, over my finances,
over my family, over my friends, over my relatives, over
my job and over my businesses.
I rebuke death, I rebuke defeat, I rebuke sickness,
and I rebuke poverty in my life in the name of Jesus.
I release life, I release healing, I release victory and I
release the covenant blessings promised to the
descendants of Abraham in my life in the name of
Jesus.
I declare victory mine over all adverse circumstances
and adversaries in the name of Jesus.
I declare healing in my mind and body and prosperity in
every area of my life in the name of Jesus.
Amen

Jehovah my father, I am prosperous and successful not simply because of my works, but because you have favoured and blessed my endeavours as you have promised.

Father it is you who have opened doors and broken down barriers which separated me from amazing opportunities. You have not only broken down barriers and open doors, you have also closed doors in my life which needed to be shut and set up barriers in places where they are needed.

Father thank you for allowing prosperity of all kinds to flood every area of my life, and I thank you for my triumph over adversities, poverty and sickness.

Lord thank you for this season of peace, safety, abundance and happiness, which you Father have brought me into.

In the name of Jesus I pray.

Amen

Lord Jesus, thank you for your forgiveness,

for all the sins I have committed and for bringing me

into your kingdom. Lord, use me to shine in this dark

world and draw those who are lost to you.

Jesus you are the risen Christ and Everlasting King,

use me Lord to save your people from death and hell,

as you have used others to draw me to you, into

freedom and life.

Eternal God and Majesty, my life I place into your

hands to use.

In the name of Jesus I pray.

Amen

Abba Father there is no one like you, never leave me or

forsake me. Forgive me, of the sins I have committed

against you, against others and against myself.
Lord I am locked in a fierce battle with my enemies and

I need your strength and your help; I need you to act on

my behalf.

Lord if you do not come to my rescue I will be lost.

Lord my God, my eyes are focused on you, my hope

I put in you, for you are the God who brings victory

and delivers those who trust in you.

Father please, respond to my prayer with urgency

and come to my aid. In the name of Jesus I ask and

pray.

Amen

Jehovah my God I come to you in the name of Jesus.

Father thank you for this day, for life, good health,

strength and my many blessings.

Father forgive me of the sins I have committed and

wash me in the blood of Jesus your son, for you have

said, "the life of the flesh is in the blood."

Protect and nurture me Father, I need your protection

and I need your counsel and guidance .

In the name of Jesus I ask pray.

Amen

Jehovah Almighty God and Father, I love you and I admire your way of thinking big and prosperous. It is your desire to prosper your holy children both materially as well as spiritually.

Father you have promised to bless whatever we do, our property and our children if we obey your instructions. You Father have promised to bless us through our tithe, as you have said if we bring our tithe to you, you Father would be faithful to your promise and would open the windows of heaven and pour out such an awesome blessing in our life we would not have room enough to contain it.

Thank you heavenly Father for honouring your promises and blessing me with perfect health and financially so that I am able to bless others according to your word.

It is in the name of Jesus I pray.

Amen

Jesus my Lord and God, it is you who have wiped away

all my tears and it is you who have been my strength

through the dark times. You have transformed

my weeping into laughter and my sadness into joy.

Lord Jesus you have not only blessed me you have also

blessed, protected and held my family together

through the rough times. Lord my God, I praise you and

I thank you our provider and deliverer.

Lord you are good and excellent in all of heaven and

earth. Lord Jesus you are wonderful and excellent in all

of heaven and earth.

In the name of Jesus I declare and pray.

Amen

Father in heaven my weeping is for a short while but I know you will bring me joy in the morning. I depend on you, I put my trust in your promise to deliver, to for provide and to promote me.

Lord remember your promise to deliver and me from all my troubles and satisfy all my needs and desires. Because of your love for me and faithfulness to me I am assured of your help.

Father thank you for acting on my prayers, on you I can depend and do depend.

In the name of Jesus I give you thanks and pray.

Amen

I declare, greater is the Holy Spirit that is in me than the

devil and demonic forces who are in the world.

I plead the blood of Jesus over my life, over my family,

over my job, over my business and over my properties.

Satan the blood of Jesus is against you in my life.

Satan the blood of Jesus is against you in my family.

Satan the blood of Jesus is against you at my

place of work.

Satan I rebuke you in the name of Jesus.

Satan I bind your activities in my life, in my family,

at my place of work, in my business and in my finances

in the name of Jesus.

Lord Jesus I loose your awesome and all-powerful

Holy Spirit in my life and upon my family in the name of

Jesus I declare these.

Amen.

Jehovah my heavenly Father, this day is ending and I thank you for bringing me and my family through it safely.

Thank you for every breath and heartbeat, for all the blessings, your grace, mercy, favour and help throughout today.

Father I ask you please to forgive me of the sins I have committed and watch over us tonight. My life and the safety of my family I leave in your hands.

In the name of Jesus I pray.

Amen

Lord Jesus thank you for this new day.

Lord I do not want to face this day alone, please be

with me and guide me.

Please protect me and give me your favour.

Be also with my loved-ones, guide, council

and protect us always, in the name of Jesus I ask.

Amen

Lord Jesus I come to you with filled with gratitude and praise. For you Lord have rebuked my enemies for my sake, and have delivered me out of all my troubles. You Lord have gone before me and have levelled all mountains, broken down barriers and removed all obstacles and have opened many doors for me so that I can live in peace and prosperity as you have promised. Lord success has truly and completely overtaken me and overwhelmed my life.

Thank you Lord Jesus my God and King, hallelujah.

Hallelujah Jesus my Lord and God, hallowed be your name.

Almighty God thank you for my promotions and blessings, thank you for my victory over death, poverty and sickness, and for coming to my rescue always.

In the name of Jesus I pray.

Amen

Lord Jesus reign in me.

Let your Holy Spirit reign in me, in its awesome power. Let your Spirit in its power explode in my life propelling me to greatness. Touch my life, inspire and encourage me and help me to conquer new territories. Lord Jesus loose my joy, loose my family from the power of the enemy, loose our minds from the lies of the enemy. Come and take control now Lord, in the name of Jesus I ask.

Amen

Jesus my Lord and God, release your Holy Spirit upon
this earth and let your Holy Spirit invade the lives of
your people all over this world.
Lord let your holy, powerful and awesome spirit
bring peace, favour from you, healing,
victory, deliverance, hope, joy, vision, power,
revelation and knowledge and both material
and spiritual blessings to the lives of your people.
In the name of Jesus I ask and pray.

Amen

Lord Jesus you are greater than all the problems that are affecting the lives of your people. Lord I ask you to invade the lives of your people and heal bodies, invade homes all over the world and take control. Strengthen, encourage and bless fathers and mothers who are struggling and who have and who are about to give up.

Lord look at the sufferings of your people and act now and remove mountains which hinder your chosen and those who have chosen you from moving forward in you and in life on this earth, please open doors to greater opportunities for your people.

Lord Jesus, please bless, heal and deliver your people.

In the name of Jesus I ask and pray.

Amen

Lord Jesus I cry out for you, come in Lord and quench

my thirst for you, you are the true and living God.

Lord you said whoever seeks you; you would let them

find you; and if we draw close to you; you will draw

closer to us.

Lord Jesus I want you to engulf my whole being. Lord

wash me with you blood and let it permeate my life and

soul. Take my life Lord and direct me, give me your

good council. Move on me Lord Jesus, I earnestly desire

your presence, do the impossible through me.

My soul cries out for and stretches out to you Lord.

Lord Jesus, please answer my call and descend upon me

and invade my life with you spirit and in your power.

In the name of Jesus I pray.

Amen

Lord Jesus, you are wonderful and awesome.

You are present in my life, I can see you and my

blessings are evidence of your presence and favour.

Yes I confess that I am incredibly blessed and favoured

and others confess it too, through their observations.

Lord I know you are in my life, but I desire more of you.

I am not satisfied with our relationship; I desire a more

profound relationship with you.

I want to see you in your glory; I want to be elevated in

you my Lord. Devour me Lord Jesus, consume me, fill

me with your glory.

Lord Jesus break loose in my life, I hunger and thirst for

more of you my God.

Hear my prayer and move now to satisfy my desires,

feed my hunger and quench my thirst for a more

profound relationship with you, Lord Jesus.

In Jesus name I ask and pray.

Amen

Lord Jesus help us, your people to see you high and lifted up, full of splendour, power and authority.

Help us to see you victorious over all things even death.

Help us to see you as the conquering Christ.

Lord you told us you can do much greater than our imagination can reach and it is an impossibility for you to fail, for you word has authority and power and must be manifested.

Lord help us to see you as you truly are, help us to stretch our imaginations and give us visions. Help us to know you, for a people who know you as you truly are will do and accomplish great exploits. Lord help us to think and think big and prosperous.

In the name of Jesus I ask and pray.

Amen

Lord Jesus forgive me of the sins I have committed
as I come into your presence. Thank you Lord for giving
me possession of this land and for helping me to
prosper in this country.

Lord than you for hiding me in the shadows of your
wings and delivering me out of all troubles victoriously.
Lord Jesus thank you for inspiration, hope, peace, your
grace, your help, good council and incredible
opportunities. Thank you Lord for renewing my mind
and uplifting my spirit. Thank you Lord Jesus, for
everything, in the name of Jesus I pray.

Amen

Lord Jesus, I was oppressed and in distress and you heard my prayers and came to my rescue. You came from heaven with the answers to resolve all the troubles I faced here on earth.

Lord thank you for coming to my rescue or I would have been lost, my troubles would have devoured me. Thank you Lord Jesus for looking beyond the sins I have committed and coming to my aid. Thank you Jesus my King and Lord and please forgive me of the sins I have committed.

In the name of Jesus I ask and pray.

Amen

Lord Jesus, you have anointed my head,

my life exudes with blessings and my mouth

is filled with praise to you.

You have made me glad Lord;

I must rejoice my Lord for you have blessed me

not only materially but with your spirit.

I must rejoice for you have made me glad.

Hallelujah Jesus, King of kings.

Hallelujah Jesus, Lord over all.

Hallelujah Jesus, Mighty and everlasting God.

Hallelujah Jesus my King.

Amen

Lord Jesus I love being in your presence. It is comforting to know that nothing can separate me from your love. Lord I love being in your presence, it gives me peace to know that you envelope me and everyone and thing which concerns me.

Lord I good to know that I am wrapped up in your love and your Holy Spirit is within me thank you for your counsel and direction. I am truly blessed that you are in my life.

Hallelujah Jesus, hallelujah Lord.

Lord I love being in your presence always.

In the name of Jesus I pray.

Amen

Lord Jesus you said you will never leave me or forsake me and as far as the east is from the west that is how far you will remove all my sins from me if only I accept you as my Lord and Saviour and turn from doing evil.

Lord Jesus I accept you as my Lord and saviour, please forgive me of the sins which I have committed. Lord I know that you heard me and have accepted me as a brother and I am now made a child of the true and living God. Now I have the right to go boldly in the presence of Almighty God to speak to him directly, no longer separated by sin.

Thank you Lord Jesus my friend and brother for your sacrifices and the privileges your suffering, death and resurrection has given to me, lead me Lord always.

It is in the name of Jesus I ask and pray.

Amen

Holy Spirit, reach deep in my soul and satisfy my great

hunger and thirst for the true and living God.

Holy Spirit, spirit of power and authority, transform my

life from the inside out, in the name of Jesus I ask.

Birth the talents which Almighty God himself have

deposited in me, which lay dormant.

Break loose in my life Holy Spirit and transform me.

In the name of Jesus I ask and pray.

Amen.

Father in heaven it is because of your mercy, grace and love why I am alive and not only alive but truly living and thriving.

Thank you Lord Jesus for teaching me and showing me the way to the Father and everlasting life. Lord it is because of your favour why I am high and lifted up.

Abba Father thank you for all which you have given to and done for me in the natural and supernatural.

Thank you for power and authority, truly I thank you for where you have brought me from and all which you have brought me through.

Now Father bring our relationship to new heights, Father you know my heart and you know my desire for you is genuine. Come closer to me Almighty God and reveal yourself to me.

In the name of Jesus I ask and pray.

Amen

Jehovah, my God I come to you in the name of Jesus.

Almighty God, help me to start and run my own

companies. Give me wisdom and inspiration,

bring me into contact with the right people and

organisations, which will help me to bring my visions

and desires into reality.

Father, help me to run these businesses profitably

and successfully and bring them to heights higher than I

could ever imagine.

Father you told me to enlarge my thinking and you

would enlarge my territory and influence. Almighty God

it is you who have given me to abilities and

opportunities to create wealth.

Father I as I am obedient to your word, I know you will

be faithful to yours.

In the name of Jesus I pray.

Amen

Heavenly Father, as a human being I tend to focus on what I do not have rather than what you have given to me and more readily believe the negative rather than the positive.

Father, help me to make the maximum use of everything that you give to me no matter how small.

Father you can do the impossible with the insignificant and insufficient, because you used two fishes and five loaves to feed thousands.

You have not given me a spirit of fear, instead you have given me a spirit of power and authority and have blessed me with a sound mind.

Father I place confidence in you, in your power and authority and I trust and obey your word.

Let my faith in your word bear much fruit in my life.

In the name of Jesus I pray.

Amen

Jehovah my Father I present this nation to you,

its people and its government. Father let your

Holy Spirit descend from heaven in power and authority

and take over. Father we need you to show us the way,

we need your direction and your authority over us.

Lord release the grip that the enemy have on our cities,

our communities, our families and myself.

Almighty God direct us, council us and take authority

over us, we need you Father, help us.

In the name of Jesus I ask and pray.

Amen

Lord Jesus, Adam was never alone for he had your company and hosts of angels. You Lord would descend from heaven and walk and talk with him in the Garden of Eden, and one day you looked and said it is not good that man should be alone, I will make a suitable companion for him.

You Lord, placed Adam in a deep sleep and created from his rib Eve and gave her to him, for them to be companions.

Father it is not good that I am alone, I need in my life right now the woman whom you have crated to be my wife and life companion. Heavenly Father right now bring into my life the woman whom you have created to be my wife.

In the name of Jesus I ask and pray.

Amen

Heavenly Father I know you are always present in my
life but yet my life feels empty and lonely.
Father, I need a family of my own to fill the void and
share my life. I earnestly desire a wife and my own
children.
Lord Jesus I look to for help, and I ask you in the name
of Jesus to bring my desires into reality.
You have promised me that I would be fruitful and have
many healthy children.
My desire is for a family of my own, please Lord Jesus
act now on my request and bring your promise and my
desire into reality Lord, for I am ready.
In the name of Jesus I ask and pray.
Amen

Jehovah you are my Father in heaven and it is because of your sacrifice why I have hope when problems and adversities arrive. It is because of your sacrifice why I am always victorious over my enemies and adversities. Father it is because of your sacrifice why I can boldly approach your the thrown of grace, love, power and authority. It is because of your sacrifice why I am separated from sickness and poverty. Heavenly Father it is because of your sacrifice why I have eternal life. Thank you for sacrificing you innocent son Jesus to give me life, freedom and authority.

Hallelujah Jehovah, my Father and God.

Hallowed be your name.

Thank you my God, in the name of Jesus I pray.

Amen.

Jehovah, my father in heaven, you told us that a people

who knows and have a relationship with you will be

strong and accomplish great things.

Father I am ambitious to both to know you more

and achieving great thing. Lord help me, direct me and

council me and help me to do and achieving great

things and move closer to you.

In the name of Jesus I ask and pray.

Amen

Jehovah, all-powerful, ever-present and omniscient
God. It is in the name of Jesus your son that I come to
you to present my request.

Father give me your favour, your grace, your help and
your protection through this day, I need you. I need the
presence and encouragement of your Holy Spirit
through today and I need your council this day.

Thank you Father for my blessings through today.

It is in the name of Jesus, your son I ask.

Amen

Hallelujah Jesus, King of kings, glorious and mighty God

who is worthy of all praise, and glory and honor.

Hallelujah Jesus, Mighty God, Everlasting Father and

Prince of Peace.

Wash me in your blood Lord, lie it permeate my mind,

body and soul.

Hallelujah King Jesus, you are King over all kings and

Lord over all, who reigns with power and authority over

all.

Hallelujah King Jesus, Lord over all, hallelujah

King Jesus.

Amen

Lord Jesus demons come not to play with us instead
they have come to kill, steal and destroy us.
Merciful God and Lord, you have given us victory and
power over all principalities and powers even those in
high positions. You have already made a way of escape
for us in all situations and from all temptations.
Lord forgive us of the evil we have done and the wrong
choices we have made and help us to see you more
clearly, so that we may place more confidence in you
and follow you, when faced with adversity and
temptations.
It is in the name of Jesus I ask and pray.
Amen

Jehovah, God of the universe and beyond.

Father let your Holy Spirit descend and capture this city.

Let your will be done through the local government,

the council and in the schools and through the police

force.

Father let your Holy Spirit invade communities, homes

and individual lives all over this city and release the

grasp that the enemy has on our society and take over.

Father lead us and give us your council and teach us

about you and your son Jesus, the Christ.

In the name of Jesus I ask and pray.

Amen

No weapon that is forged to harm the people of

Jehovah the highest God will accomplish its purpose.

You Lord have built a fence around your people to

protect us from the attacks of the enemy.

Whenever the enemy comes in we know that you will

use these adversities to lift us higher and make us

stronger in the end.

Lord your sacrifices and love for us has made us more

than conquerors, thank you Lord Jesus.

It is in the name of Jesus I pray.

Amen

Lord Jesus, you told us to pray for our leaders,

so Lord I lift up this government and its head to you.

It is you who put governments in place and it is you

who remove them.

It is in your hands, under your power and authority that

the mind of our head of state and leader of this

government and the head of ever nation's government

rests, and you can direct them wherever you choose.

Lord Jesus, I ask you in the name of Jesus to take control

of the mind of this nation's leader and head of state.

Cause the leader of our government to govern well;

council him and surround him with good council,

inform him protect him and his family.

Let your will be done through him and his subordinates;

cause his government to put into effect policies that will

not only benefit this nation but the world.

It is in your hands that I leave the government of this

nation.

In the name of Jesus I pray.

Amen

Lord Jesus, since we become the company we keep

thank you Lord for the sphere of people whom you

have brought and those whom you are yet to bring into

my life. People whom you have chosen not only to have

a positive social, financial and material impact on my life

but also spiritual.

People who will strengthen my relationship with you

and expand my knowledge and views of you.

Lord Jesus, thank you for these people and help me to

make the maximum use of the benefits which having

made the acquaintance of such people can bring.

Thank you Lord for blessing my life through these your

chosen.

In the name of Jesus I pray.

Amen

I declare in the name of Jesus any weapon forged harm me will never prosper in what it was designed to achieve instead it will be a blessing rather than a curse or hindrance and every tong that accuses me will be condemned.

My enemies are defeated; every enemy that have and will rise against me is already defeated and every mountain which is before me will be levelled.

By the wounds of Jesus I am healed of all sickness and is made well.

Christ Jesus has made me more than a conquer and his Holy Spirit lives within me, his spirit which is greater than all, lives within me.

In the name of Jesus I declare.

Amen

Jehovah, my Father and God I ask you in the name of
Jesus to forgive me of the sins I have committed.
Father thank you for making me into the man I am
today and for your continued work in improving me.
Thank you for vision and self belief, as you know it is
important that I believe in myself as I in you.
Father I have endured many dark and lean years, thank
you for being my light, my strength, my council and my
provider through those years and even now.
Father thank you for where you have brought me from
and I appreciate where I am now in life at this moment
and thank you for the heights which you are carrying me
to. Father my courage comes from knowing you are
always with me; guiding, helping and protecting me.
Jehovah my Father and God thank you for everything.
In the name of Jesus I pray.

Amen

Lord Jesus, the chastisement for our peace was laid upon you. You know the suffering and sacrifice it took to give us peace, so Lord I ask you in the name of Jesus to let peace reign in my home.

Let peace reign between me and my wife.

Let peace reign between me and my children.

Let peace reign between my wife and our children.

I declare peace in the name of Jesus in my home.

I declare peace in my family and I rebuke every demonic and human influence which tries to create division, hatred and animosity in my family.

In the name of Jesus I declare and pray.

Amen

Jehovah, omnipresent, omniscient, omnipotent and
eternal God. Your words have power and are true,
they will never return to you without completing their
purpose.

Father you have declared to heaven and earth that it is
not good for man to be aloe and you will make a
suitable partner for him.

Father look on me, a lonely man and let you words be
established in my life. Father bring into my life right
now the woman whom you have promised to bless me
with to rid me of loneliness.

Father you have declared that whoever finds a wife
finds a good thing and have your favour.

All-mighty God and Father, favour me and bring my
spouse which you have promised into my life, right now.

In the name of Jesus I ask.

Amen

Lord Jesus, there are so many people out there who need your help and your presence in their lives. There are so many searching for answers only you can give.

So many turn to drugs, to gangs, to violence, to cults, to witchcraft and so many other avenues; searching for answers, searching for peace, searching for purpose, searching for a place to belong; Lord all these you can fulfil.

Lord Jesus, let your Holy Spirit descend upon us all right now and show us the way to you. The way to peace, to everlasting life and to the true living and God. Lord, let your Holy Spirit fall now, let your Holy Spirit invade now, let you Holy Spirit lead and teach us now.

In the name of Jesus I ask and pray.

Amen

I declare in the name of Jesus that I am the head and not the tail. I am above only and not beneath and where ever I go I will prosper and what ever I do will prosper.

I declare in the name of Jesus, Satan and all demons defeated in my life. I declare and release life in my life in the name of Jesus. I declare myself victorious over every adversity and adversaries which come against in Jesus name. I declare and release healing in my life in Jesus name. I declare and release joy in my life in Jesus name I declare in the name of Jesus all my todays and tomorrows blessed. I release the covenant blessings to the descendants of Abraham in my life I declare in the name of Jesus that I am a child of Jehovah the true and living God.

Amen

Jesus my Lord and God thank you for being faithful
to your promises concerning the tithe.
Lord you told me if I bring the tithe to you, you
would rebuke the devil and his demons for my sake
and you would throw open the windows of heaven
and pour out through those windows such
a blessing in my life I would not have
room enough to contain it all.
Lord Jesus I have been obedient to your instruction
and you have been faithful to your promises.
Thank you for rebuking Satan and his demons and
my enemies for my sake and for releasing the
covenant blessings to the descendants of
Abraham in my life. Thank you for protecting me,
for counselling me, for directing me, and the grace,
mercy and favour you have given to me.
In the name of Jesus I pray.
Amen

Lord Jesus, I will not let my knowledge of the sins which
I have committed stop me from coming to you or
praising you. You are Lord over all and king over all
kings.

Hallelujah Jesus, hallelujah Lord,

hallelujah Mighty God, King over all kings.

You are the one who have delivered me out of all my

troubles. You are the one who lifted me up when I was

down. You have always been there for me during the

good and bad times helping me, supporting me,

counselling me and correcting me.

Hallelujah Jesus, hallelujah Lord,

hallelujah Jesus, hallelujah my Lord.

Thank you for all that you have done for me

in the past, present and future, thank you Lord Jesus.

In the name of Jesus I pray.

Amen

Lord Jesus my God as you have promised, you have restored to me the years that the enemy had stolen or destroyed.

Lord Jesus, please help me not to waste this time you have given back to me, help me Lord to live wisely.

You can see the future and you control all things and my life I gladly leave in your hands.

Lord Jesus you have given me life and have sustained me all these years, please help me to live and be fruitful.

It is in the name of Jesus I ask and pray.

Amen

Jesus, Lord Jesus I must praise and honour you.

I acknowledge that is you Lord, who has made me glad.

It is you Lord who has made me glad even in the midst

of terrible trouble, it is you who has made me glad.

Hallelujah Jesus my Lord and God

Hallelujah Jesus my friend and brother

Hallelujah Jesus my provider and deliverer.

Lord you are excellent and wonderful from eternity

to eternity.

Hallelujah Jesus, my Lord and God

You are excellent Lord, you are excellent and wonderful.

Hallelujah Jesus, hallelujah Lord, it is you who has made

me glad and who have already delivered safely and

victoriously me out of these present troubles.

Hallelujah Jesus, hallelujah Lord,

it is you who has made me glad

It is in the name of Jesus I pray.

Amen

Hallelujah Jesus, hallelujah Lord, you are truly excellent.

Lord you are truly wonderful and marvellous and I
thank you for this season of peace and prosperity
which I am now living in.

Lord thank you for hiding me in your shadows and
holding me and keeping me safe in your loving arms.

Lord Jesus thank you for looking beyond the sins I have
committed and loving me and comforting me when I
am afraid and strengthening me when I am weak.

Lord you are truly a wonderful and excellent.

Hallelujah Jesus, hallelujah my Lord, hallowed be
your name.

In the name of Jesus I pray.

Amen

Lord Jesus hallowed be your name.

Lord Jesus I come to you asking for your forgiveness

of all the sins which I have committed.

Thank you for your grace, mercy and love which you

have freely and unselfishly given to me.   I thank you for

all the blessings which you have allowed to come to me,

including your favour and protection.

Lord most of all, I thank you for teaching me your ways,

for direction and council and for sacrificing your life to

save mine and bringing me into the kingdom of Jehovah

who is the true God.

Lord I thank you for forgiving me of all the sins which I

have committed and for being a true friend and also a

teacher.

Hallelujah Jesus, you are my Lord and friend.

It is in the name of Jesus that I pray.

Amen

Lord Jesus you have borne all our sins. You were afflicted and wounded for sins we have committed, you were bruised for our iniquities and chastised so that we would have peace. By the wounds which were inflicted upon you, we are healed of all sicknesses.

All of us like sheep had gone astray; we all had gone our own way in disobedience to the word of the true and living God.

Through his love for us he sacrificed you Lord Jesus and placed all our sins upon you to pay the price, which is death.

Lord Jesus you have redeemed us from the curse of the law, being made a curse for us: for it is written, "Cursed is every one that hangs on a tree."

Lord Jesus today you are no longer on the cross or buried in the grave. You are the risen Christ, the conquering Christ who has all power and authority over everything in the natural and supernatural; even over death itself.

Even now you make intercessions for us to the Father.

Lord Jesus thank you for you love and faithfulness and please forgive me of my trespasses.

In the name of Jesus I ask and pray.

Amen